This book is dedicated to my children Karin and Erich and my dear four grandchildren, all four boys, Scott, Jack, Peter and Luke. The stories it contains are intended to keep alive memories and meanings of my life as a reflection of my personal experiences.

ISBN 978-1-105-32818-3

Well, so many, many friends have told me to write a book about my experiences in life and I didn't know where to start. At my winter residence in Myrtle Beach at a cocktail party one of my friends mentioned that he belonged to a writer's group. I asked him how to start my book and he told me to write short stories, whatever came to my mind; later on I could put them together for a book. That would be much easier to handle. Al promised to send me some of his own stories after our winter stay in the south.

I received several of his stories; on top of it he also sent me a few of his friend's stories. His friend, like me, also immigrated to the USA after the war from Germany. His name is Hans. Some of their stories reported war experiences which were interesting, coming from an American former soldier and a German soldier. All of a sudden my memories of the war came back to me, which were buried deep inside of me for a long time.

The below stories have been given to me by Al and Henry and helped me to begin my book. Thank you to both of you for giving your permission so that I am able to start my book with your stories.

From A. J. Booth:

INTERLUDE

Everyone had shed his socks and pulled on dry ones. I continued to rub one foot and then the other between both hands to warm my cold and tired feet. I slipped on a second pair of socks. That should do it, I thought as I fell back on the bed. That's better. Warm feet and a few hours sleep will do wonders for the morale of this ragged platoon.

The trucks that delivered us from Le Havre had dropped us two days ago and we'd been walking all day, each day, since. We hadn't been told where we were, or where we were headed.
Overcast December skies and long periods of hiking in the rain added to our disorientation and frustration.

Where we were right now, in someone' s farmhouse, was all that counted. It mattered not if this haven was in France, Belgium or Timbuctoo. It was dry and warm with room to stretch out and get some shuteye. We knew we'd be back on the road early in the morning, but for now warm feet and sleep came first. The room grew quiet.

"Let's go! Let's go! Everybody outside! Move it!" Lombardy shouted from the foot of the stairs. "Lets go! Damn it! On the double!"

Moans and groans rose from the dozen weary soldiers sprawled around the small bedroom. As they gained their feet, soul-felt profanity joined the buckling on of ammo belts and various other gear. Feet, newly clad in dry socks just one hour earlier, were shoved into still wet boots.

Go? We just got here! What in hell is the hurry? We haven't even had a chance to get warm. Why can't we stay here tonight. God? I pleaded. Seems like Sgt. Lombardy outranks God in this forsaken spot. Probably thinks he does. Damn all sergeants!

Move out? For the first time in weeks we're inside a real shelter. I'd sell my soul for just a couple of hours out of the cold rain and mud. Our shot at sleep was gone. Outside, as night fell, the drop in temperature changed the daylong rain to sleet. A howling wind drove it crackling against the small window at the head of the bed.

I had just a glimpse of the elderly couple standing beside the kitchen table as our unit took over their farmhouse. Obviously worried, and unsure of our intentions, they had little choice but to watch quietly as we occupied their home. Later I would wonder if they had similarly "hosted" German soldiers in the days or hours just before we arrived.

As we walked in, some of the guys fell into the first chairs they spotted. Others stretched out on the floor around the warm stove. A few claimed chairs at the kitchen table, dropped their heads on crossed forearms and were asleep. We were a cold, wet and exhausted bunch leery of what lay ahead.

I joined the group heading up the narrow staircase in search of beds. The room we found was sparsely furnished, just a double bed, two straight chairs and one small table under a window. It was immaculate when we walked in. What it would look like when we left, I didn't want to think about. After shedding ammo belts, canteens, helmets and weapons, we tended to our feet.

Three of us lay crosswise on the bed, our feet sticking out into space.

The others, some lucky enough to find blankets or quilts, stretched out on the floor.

Sgt. Lombardy bellowed once more from below. We grabbed our helmets and rifles and headed for the stairs. Curiosity stopped me halfway across the room. There, chest-high on the chimney wall, a small wooden door with a knobbed pull, begged to be opened. I obliged. Inside hung two great-looking smoked hams. We stared at them. We looked at each other. Someone said, "Leave them," and I quickly closed the door.

Our sergeant stood at the foot of the stairs. "Everybody will make a contribution," he ordered, nodding toward the center of the room. The farmer and his wife watched as each one placed several cans of "C" rations on the table before stepping out into the night. The dark green cans of our much-maligned rations covered the entire table. I was the last to contribute. At the door I looked back and saw the woman reaching to embrace Sgt. Lombardy. Her husband wiped his eyes with his shirtsleeve.

1 guess Lombardy is not the S.O.B. we had come to know. Maybe he's just a hard-ass because he thinks we need it. I still suspect he has a bit of a mean streak.

Two minutes later he joined us in the cold darkness. The sleet had eased up. "Move out!" our sergeant shouted and we headed down the road.

JOHN SKEVINGTON

Each Christmas season something triggers my memory of John Skevington and the day the Germans ambushed our platoon on a wooded hillside in Belgium's Ardennes Forest late in December 1944.

This year's flashback surprised me during a post-lunch walk with my brother Don in the woods behind my daughter's house. The trigger, matted layers of wet decomposing leaves, lay beneath our feet. They carpeted the stand of trees, bare and black-wet with winter moisture. I was 19 again in full field gear with the base plate of a 60 millimeter mortar strapped to my hip as my unit scuffed through the sodden leaves in a foreign wood.

As I bent to step over a large fallen branch, a bullet snapped past my left ear. Behind me John fell, instantly dead. I dropped to the ground next to him as more bullets slammed into the trees and ground around us. John's blood spread and blackened the damp matted leaves beneath his head. His pale blue eyes stared at me in quiescent contrast to the chaos of gunfire, shouts and cries for help.

The attack ended as suddenly as it had begun. Our guys, wits recovered, pulses harnmering, raked the undergrowth at the base of the hill with their M-Is and Browning Automatics. They were too late. The Germans had hit and run. I slipped the strap of the mortar barrel from John's shoulder on to mine and with the rest of our unit, the unscathed helping the wounded, scrambled back to our previous dug-in positions several hundred yards behind us. We realized the Nazi bastards would be coming at us when darkness fell.

John's body and others lay in the woods for two days before the enemy gave up attempts to overrun our position. As we moved out in pursuit of the Germans we passed the spot of the ambush. I didn't know if I could stand to see John, so I looked the other way.

I see him now at all my Christmastimes. To this day I am profoundly sad and angry when I think of why and how his life ended, of his future denied. In my marrow

I know that when we walked into that ambush a hidden German soldier had me, not John Skevington, in the cross hairs of his rifle.

From Henry Boessll:

MY FIRST ELECTION

On January 20, 1933 - a recent note in the newspaper defined that date, I would not have remembered - my parents went to vote. The voting hall was one of the rooms in the elementary school which **I** was going to attend the following fall as my mother was telling me. It was the Schule an der Tuerkenstrasse in Munich, Germany, and the election was to make Adolf Hitler the Reichskanzler (General Chancellor) of Germany. At the time I did not understand what the election was about, of course, being only five years of age, but I do remember this:

I was allowed to enter the voting room with my parents. Upon entering each voter was .given a sheet of paper. The sheet had two circles printed 'on it, one large with the word JA! in it, the other circle much smaller, saying NEIN!!. In the room there was a regular table where the voters placed their sheets down and marked an "X" in one of the circles. Several voters were present when we were in the room. Anyone could watch. Off against one wall was a' stand, like a lectern that had a black curtain around the upper part "for those who did not wish to be observed" as my parents explained, I did not see that stand being used.

After the "X" had been marked the ballot sheet was folded in half and the voters lined up at another table with several men sitting behind large books, checking names and addresses, one voter at a time. At the end of this table was a large, cloth-draped enclosure, taller than .a person, and after the men who checked the names and addresses had marked off the books and called out the registration number, the ballot was dropped into an opening on top of that tall enclosure.

As we left the 'school, two men stopped everyone and without asking questions, stuck a lapel-pin on each voter's jacket or dress. The pin read "JA!". Nobody refused that pin.

At home I overheard my parents say that in that tall enclosure there was probably a man who wrote the registration number on the ballot so they would know who voted "NEIN". A year or two later, my parents would not have discussed that with me around anymore.

A CHILD'S PLAY

Many a summer Sunday morning my parents and I bicycled to a forest on the outskirts of Munich, away from the crowds and the bustle of the city. Mother spread out a blanket and father strung up- the hammock from two trees. I set up my toy train and used the many twisting roots along the forest floor as railroad tracks. The breeze brushing through the pines, an- occasional bird call, the-slow, rhythmic grunting of the hammock's ropes, the resin smell of the tree bark reminiscent of incense, all had an entrancing effect. Lunch was tea and jelly pancakes. From this oasis of peace and comfort my toy train took me-to the fantastic places that only exist for the very young.

I always insisted that we-pick a spot close-to the-clear-cut area where- actual railroad tracks ran so I could see the trains rumble by. This close to the city station they traveled at reduced speed, and the engineers leaned out the steam engines' windows checking the signal lights.

Whenever a train' approached I ran to- the-edge-of the clearing, stood on a small rise and, making sure that the engineer was looking my way, raised my hand in the smart Hitler salute they had just taught us in first grade. The engineers always returned the salute. They wouldn't dare *not* to respond: The time of their passing and the-number on the-engine would make-it easy to track down a railroad employee who was not properly enthusiastic about the new regime.

To my disappointment, my parents, especially my father, did not encourage me in this micro-demonstration. Many years later I understood. Father had been a soldier in World War I1. Now he- saw through the glitter which so dazzled most people.

But he never spoke about his thoughts. He didn't dare to.

THE BEGINNING

The big day had arrived.

Vacation was over and this was my first day **in** a new school.

It was a pleasant, peaceful late summer day. Women had placed their feather bedding on the open window sills to expose them to the sun.

As I walked the new route I heard the Munich radio station from the open apartment windows.

My mother, a seamstress, had made me a new pair of knickerbockers, and I wore them proudly even though they still were not really a part of me.

I was full of anxiety. The switch to a secondary school had not been my idea. My teacher and my parents had made that decision for me and so with trepidations this shy eleven-year old kid was now on the path to a higher education.

My mind on the challenges before me, the radio program was way in the back of my consciousness.

Until, suddenly, the announcer's words pierced my thoughts: " ... but the German Armed Forces have repelled the invaders and are presently matching into Poland, driving the agressors before them ... "

It was the first day of September, 1939. World War II had just begun.

THE FINAL DAYS

In January 1944 the three 5th grade classes of the Gisela Oberschule (an all-boys high-school) in Munich were assembled in the gymnasium for a special announcement. The Principal informed us that as of the following Monday (January 10) we were assigned to the anti-aircraft unit located in Engelschalking on the outskirts of Munich, where we would be considered "Luftwaffenhelfer" (Air Force Auxiliaries). From then on we lived in barracks and did soldiers' duties manning the anti-aircraft equipment . I turned 16 two months later; others were younger yet.

I always had wanted to fly an airplane, had volunteered for the Luftwaffe (the German Airforce) and after several tests, had been accepted. For lack of fuel they did not draft me immediately. However, there was preparation in the form of glider pilot training. Another member of my unit (I'll call him Hans - his real name I cannot recall) also had been accepted and while we both were away learning to fly sailplanes our Flak unit was transferred to Augsburg where the Messerschmidt aircraft factory took savage bombings almost every day.

After completing the glider course - in mid-winter - Hans and I were informed that our unit was now in Augsburg, but when we got there - partly by bicycle because there were few trains still operating - they literally sent us home. The barracks had been all3 but annihilated a few days before and there was no way they could put us up. All shelters were overcrowded with the homeless and wounded. We returned to Munich with orders to spend every other night as auxiliary policemen in the local precinct to help maintain order after air raids. All raids by then took place during the day, though, and I never actually got involved in any night duty.

We settled into the basic survival type of life that still went on in the crippled city. There was no- school, hardly any food, and almost no transportation. The few trucks that brought supplies ran on wood-gas, which made the trucks stink, and required that the ashes be dumped out of the on-board converters every so often. Piles of ashes lined the streets like horse droppings *in* the times before the automobile. Streetcars had stopped operating long ago, bicycle tires were replaced with wire-tied rows of bottle-corks, or rode-directly on the bare wheel rims. The only public transportation still running in a fashion was what we called the "Gauleiter", an allusion to the highest political office holder in the district, through whose graces this unique transportation was made available. And it was a sight: A narrow gauge railroad, steam-engine propelled, with makeshift benches on the flat cars. The ties and rails were- simply laid on top of the street or rubble, and the tracks could be quickly rerouted as required after bomb raid damages. At intersections they dumped piles of dirt to form ramps for other vehicles to cross. These slow, smoke belching mini-railroads had been used at large construction sites in normal times. Now the wood-fired steam engines and their little open wagons became-the-only public means of transportation, rain or snow, dust or soot.

Some people still went to work. Iknow my father tried daily but did not always succeed to get transportation to the suburb where he worked.

Most of our time was spent simply surviving. We-pulled half-burnt timber from collapsed buildings, sawed and chopped them to firewood size chunks. Coal trucks going around curves often lost a little- coal and that had to be- gotten before others found it. Mother scrounged around for food whenever a rumor implied that something was available somewhere. And we spent a lot of time salvaging (stealing!) water pipes from bombed-out houses which we needed to-rebuild the bomb-damaged lines that led to our own tenement house. This saved us several times when incendiary bombs set parts of our house on fire.

My father, who was 70 years old at that time, had a permanent assignment with the equivalent of Civil Defense, helping to repair damaged houses whenever he couldn't get to work. And of course, after bomb raids there were buried people to rescue, damaged houses to evacuate, fires to put out.

Secretly I listened to the Voice of Ameriea on the crystal set earphones, but only my parents knew about this source of news that was so different from the official broadcasts. Our superintendent's 14-year old son had mentioned to friends that his father listened to the Voice of America at times. One night the Gestapo just hauled the man away and he was never heard from again. Dachau concentration camp, we supposed, but not even his wife ever found out.

Early in April 1945 - shortly after my 17th birthday - I received a notice in the mail that I had been assigned to the Waffen-SS a special sub-unit of the SS - the dreaded political military police who dominated all other branches of the armed forces and who had the authority to induct anyone regardless of other obligations or assignments. I was to report for duty in Reutte, Austria.

Only my mother knew about that note, and with shaking voices we decided to ignore that notice. With all the bomb- raids it could easily have gotten lost. From the Voice-of America I knew that it was only a matter of a few weeks before the Allied troops would march into Munich, so I took the gamble and just stayed put. Those-were tense-weeks. Had they caught me I would have been immediately executed. I knew that and so did my mother. But it could have been much worse had I obeyed the- draft notice, as I learned later.

On May 1st, 1945, the Allies rolled into Munich and the bombing stopped. No-one who has not lived through these times will understand the relief, and yet the uncertainty about what was to come. We expected the Allies to be similar to the Nazis. Or could we trust their propaganda broadcasts? What would they do? Go through every house- and check for Nazi signs? I glued a five-point paper star over the Swastika symbol on our radio. Hitler's "Mein Kampf', which my father had been given by his employer at one of his service anniversaries, had gone the way of toilct paper long ago, the pages hidden in the bathroom in case of unexpected visitors ...

As it turned out, we-were-spared most of what we-had feared. The Americans behaved very well toward us civilians and in retrospect we realized that we were very lucky not to be in any of the other occupation- zones, particularly the- Russian.

But back to the final days.

Eventually I met Hans again who had not dared disobey his draft notice and made it somehow to Reutte as directed. There he and many others were greeted by a group of SS troopers. Their civilian ID's were taken away - always the first act of induction into the services. In place of uniforms they were given Swastika armbands. Then each was handed a bazooka, and one bazooka was fired to demonstrate the proper use of this weapon. Next they were trucked toward Memmingen (south-west of Munich) and told to march westward through the woods until they encountered the advancing American forces. They were-to fire-their weapons at the-tanks to hopefully stop or at least retard their advance. The SS with their trucks stayed behind.

The first instinct of those youngsters was to run back and try to make it home, but they knew what the SS would do if they were captured. So in small groups they pretended to run to the west until the SS could no longer see them, then they circled back. The SS had anticipated that maneuver and promptly caught a bunch of them, including Hans.

Asked why they were running away they answered that they thought this was the correct direction (they had no leader, no compass). Of the group, several had thrown away their bazookas. Hans, luckily, was one of those who in the excitement had forgotten that he was still carrying his weapon. Those who still had their bazookas were harshly redirected by the SS, but the others - Hans mentioned six to eight - were treated as deserters and hanged right there. Then the SS on their trucks retreated further into the mountains.

Hans had run deeper into the woods and got separated from his buddies. All alone he emerged on the west edge of the forest, walked to a road and, still holding onto his bazooka, waited in the ditch for the enemy tanks to arrive. First he thought to let them pass - maybe they would not detect him. Then he saw foot soldiers walking besides the tanks. Surely they would not miss him. Feeling finally save from the SS, he-ripped off his Swastika armband, hid it and the bazooka in some bushes, then he got up on his shaky legs and raised his arms as high as he could. It must have-been a sight. An undernourished boy, scared almost out of his wits, popping out of a roadside ditch in front of a US Army tank column.

The totally unexpected happened! The soldiers, after verifying that he was alone, made Hans sit on top of the leading tank, gave him candy and offered cigarettes, and so advanced through the woods in which the other buddies were hidden. Luckily none of them ever fired his bazooka. When the US soldiers saw the bodies dangling from the trees, Hans in laborious school English explained what had happened. He did not recall the soldiers' reactions except that many heads were shaken in disbelief.

Thus ended the military service of one of many reluctant soldiers, only hours after he was outfitted with a token uniform and a weapon. But there is more. Not being in possession of civilian ID papers he was considered a POW. And since at that time there were more POW's than the US forces could keep and guard in Europe, he was shipped per boat to the USA and wound up in a Texas prison camp. There he was taken daily to a farm and had to help with the chores under the direction of the farmer. The farmer was of German ancestry himself and took a liking to shy Hans. He also had a pretty daughter, and eventually Hans wound up as the farmer's son-in-law. But first he had to be officially released and then apply for immigration papers. So Hans was transported back to Germany as POW, released, then - with the farmer as sponsor - he applied for a visa, and eventually he and the farmer's daughter got married.

Strange how fate works. Had I followed the draft notice instructions, I could have become that farmer's son-in-law; or a tree ornament near Memmingen. As it turned out I still carried my passport - declaring me a civilian - and was always turned free at the many check points set up in Munich during the first months of occupation. I even worked for the US Army later, and eventually emigrated to the States. But that's another chapter.

FIRST IMPRESSIONS

Shortly after my arrival in the USA in 1955-1 visited the- Public Unemployment Office in Newark, NJ, confident to find a good job in this land of opportunity. After a short wait I was ushered into the office- of a caseworker, not much older than myself (27) and obviously Jewish. He also had a Polish sounding name. Immediately my heart sank. Even though I had been-too young to have been actively involved in any Nazi atrocities, I had come from Germany and in 1955 the terror that had come to-light after the end of WW II was still very fresh on everyone's mind.

The gentleman treated me very nicely. During the ensuing conversation, me being as tense as could be, he told me that most of his family had perished in German concentration camps; his father, mother and a sister, as I recall. He- had somehow managed to be smuggled out of Germany just in time.

As he told me his story with deep emotion I felt myself physically shrinking and would have liked nothing better than to disappear entirely. This man certainly had no reason in the world to lift a finger on my behalf. He- had every justification for hating me, and while I sat there listening my mind raced on to what I would do next. Surely the Public Employment Office; with this man on the staff, would never line me up for a decent job.

However, a day or two after the interview the young man called to tell me that he had enlisted me in an aptitude test. This special test was really meant for people who had been out of work for more than six months but he had enlisted me anyway. After the four hour test he referred me to a company who hired me as laboratory assistant. Within a year they even paid for my evening courses in the Newark College of Engineering. I stayed with that firm until they were- bought out by a competitor and moved out of state eight years later

It is no exaggeration to say that due to the assistance of this young Jew I had a very good start in this country - and I will never forget!

Trudy's story:

I was born in Berlin, Germany on June 18, 1926. We lived in a nice suburb of Berlin, Spandau, surrounded by lakes and woods. When I was six years old, I was blessed with a little baby sister named Irmi. From then on, our parents took us each year for summer vacation to the Baltic Sea in Ahlbeck.

We had a lovely childhood. Mom stayed home with us and Dad was a police officer – very strict, but couldn't do enough for us. He built us a dollhouse, a Kasperle theater, and went on hikes with us through the woods. We all went swimming together, flying kites. On Sundays, he cooked us our meals while Mom made great cakes for the weekend. Our neighbors were all our age group, so we had many friends to play with.

My mom lost her parents very early in life. They lived in Königsberg, Ostpreußen, now Poland. She then was raised in Berlin by her aunt. My dad came from a big family with ten brothers and one sister. His father was a butcher, so food was no problem. In Germany, you don't invite people for a party; you just go with a gift. That was so much fun. When our birthdays came, Mom prepared lots of food in advance. She baked lots of delicious cakes, prepared various salads and sandwiches, and we were anxious to open the door when the bell rang, never knowing who would show up. Mom usually prepared for thirty to fifty people. Uncles, aunts, cousins and friends appeared on the door steps with great gifts. Of course in turn, we were also

Wedding photo of my parents July 25, 1925
Erich Jagode and Gretchen Koehler

Whole family at the wedding

Dad and Mother on the right with Trudy and Mom's family

My parents with me

Vacations with friends and family at the Baltic Sea
1928 and 1929

Each year at our Baltic Sea Vacation, my family rented a sailboat. This is about 1930.

1933

This is Trudy with her baby sister Irmi

(Later Irmi's married name was Laule.)

First day of school with schultuete, a cone filled with cookies, candy and little books given to German children at the conclusion of their first day at school.

Weverstr. 10 where we lived when I was a child.

very busy visiting for birthdays and holidays. There was always a big party somewhere without any invitations.

As an example of how important birthdays were for us, I am including here a letter I received for my birthday in 1997 (in translation): from my sister from Vienna Austria, where she lived with her husband Sep.

June 18th 1997
When we harvest strawberries and the asparagus stands high in Werder, I always knew that an important day was coming. Mom baked cake in our little portable oven, and both you and I would shake it well to make sure that the cake would turn out really gooey.
Mom never found out why.
Dad carried chairs from the Englers and from Mrs. Haack to provide seating

for all the many friends, aunts and uncles, and lots of cousins.
We were celebrating Trudy's birthday.
How wonderful our birthday celebrations always used to be.
Now the local strawberries are offered at the market and wonderful fresh asparagus. It must be Trudy's birthday.
I remember persons that have changed us and formed us,
or the power of a heartfelt prayer by which we felt invigorated.
Mom and Dad taught us to pray.
To remember our own uniqueness, this impossibility to substitute one for the other, can give us strength, because each one of us, you and I , are not just anybody but a special person, one that never was before and never again will be. Let us use this strength to continue to live.
May you have a wonderful birthday in the circle of your family, friends, and neighbors. Get well, use all your strength which we have received from Mom and Dad. We love you and think of you and wish you a happy new year of your life without pain,
Very dear greetings to all who make this day a beautiful one for you.
My dear sister-heart, may this Sacher Torte taste great to you which is sent fresh from the house of Sacher.
Your always loving Motte,
Much love, your Sepp

When my grandma's birthday came, (Grandpa died early), the children hired a big hall to have everybody come and celebrate. That was a big gathering with all my cousins, aunts and uncles. I do miss the big family get-together very much.

My parents were great to introduce us to many sport activities: skiing, ice skating, roller skating, tennis, sailing, row-boat club and bicycling. There was never a boring minute. We also had piano lessons to show off whenever we had visitors -- and that was often.

Christmas time was fairyland. During the Advent time we went with our parents to the Christmas market. The top one was in Alexanderplatz, huge and well-known in Berlin and its surrounding areas. Christmas Eve my sister Irmi and I had to stay out of the living room. That day the Christmas tree was bought and put up in the living room. From then on, my parents were busy in there. They decorated the tree and put the gifts underneath. When it got dark, we were called in. The real candles were all burning on the tree and the sparklers were hanging also on the tree bursting into beautiful stars. It was an unforgettable wonderland year after year. The tree was freshly cut that day, therefore no danger. Once the sparklers were out, Santa Claus knocked on the door, was let in and my sister Irmi and I had to recite a poem to Santa Claus, before he handed out his gifts. Then we had to go and play the piano and all of us sang Christmas carols. Then we were allowed to open the presents and enjoy eating from the "Bunte Teller" a big plate for each of us with nuts, tangerines, apples, oranges, and lots of cookies and chocolates. I always had to hide mine; my sister loved to take away the goodies. Christmas day we always had a big goose and invited lonely people like widows or sick people to join us. The second holiday, which is still in effect in Germany now, we either visited people or had visitors in our home.

My parents told me that after World War I (1914-1918) there was not much work to be found. Unemployment was at an all time high. Inflation was rampant, a loaf of bread costs millions, workers carried their weekly salaries home in backpacks which did not even pay for a pound of meat. Soon payday came daily make it possible for the workers to to lug home the load of worthless bills. After 1928 one could read signs, saying “Family father with four children will take any job!” War veterans sat on the street corner and tried to sell rubber bands and matches.

Almost eight million hungry men in Berlin without a job opened their ears for the news of Adolf Hitler with promises of jobs. When the good old Reichspresident von Hindenburg resigned to Hitler on January 30, 1933, people found work rapidly. Within six years of having a better life with jobs, the Second World War started with unbelievable death and destruction.

September 1st, 1939, one heard on the radio that the soldiers marched into Poland, the beginning of World War II. We had known it was coming. I was 13 years old.

From 10 years of age on all girls had to belong to the BDM (Bund Deutscher Mädchen) organization of girls. We all had to wear uniforms and march to the drums. I still remember May first, the National Holiday of the Olympic Stadium, where boys in their uniforms and us girls in ours had to stay for Hitler driving around in his open car shaking hands with the "Hitler-Jugend" (Hitler Youth). We were so impressed when he shook hands with some of us including me. We were children; we didn't know better. "Our Führer" (leader), shook hands with me. I came home excited to tell my parents. They didn't seem to share my excitement too much -- why?

My dad came home one day and told my mother that he was approached by Nazi's to join that organization. If not, he would be demoted in his rank as a top police officer. He went back with the answer "no" and the demotion took place. They couldn't fire him; they needed every man in the Police department!

The day after "Kristallnacht" (November 9-10, 1938)) my parents and I went shopping and saw all the stores with broken windows and people walking around with a pin saying JEW. My mom had tears in her eyes and started to talk. My father stopped her by whispering not to say anything. At this time you had no idea who was a Nazi and would arrest you. The reason my mom was so upset was that we had a Jewish family doctor who used to come to the house at any hour, if necessary. We considered him part of the family.

When the bombardment got intense (1943), all

schools were closed in Berlin and families with young children had to be evacuated to the country to escape from Berlin. Many school classes were moved as a whole. My parents did not like that idea; my sister was only 10 years old then.

For many years, we had gone to Thüringen as a family every fall for a week on vacation. My parents had found a beautiful guesthouse surrounded by mountains in a little village. The owners were farmers and the food they served was outstanding. In the fall we went through the woods and gathered a lot of mushrooms. My mom sat outside in a beautiful garden with vines hanging over the sitting areas, full of grapes, to clean the mushrooms, put them on a string and hang them in the sun to dry. The whole year we had delicious meals at home with the dried mushrooms. While Mom was cleaning mushrooms, my dad went out with the farmer to get all the wonderful ripe plums from the trees and my little sister Irmi enjoyed feeding all the animals while I helped. Thc owners of the guesthouse had two daughters close to us in age; we became close friends. They also had two sons.

It was a typical family business, hard working people, so very kind. We all became good friends during our years of vacationing at their place. So when the time of evacuation for the small children took place my parents contacted the Geyers and asked if they could send my sister Irmi to their place rather than a camp. They agreed and it was a big relief for my parents to know that my ten year old sister would have good care in their place. So we had to say goodbye, which was very, very difficult. There were no phones, of course, so we wrote lots of letters and cards back and forth. It was a train ride of five hours, so between my mom and me, we visited once in awhile and were happy to see that she was part of Geyer's family.

I never forgot one of my visits to my sister. Trains were overfilled, people were hanging on outside and my parents bought me a ticket first class for safety reasons. I was a teenager and in first class were lots of young officers. The first class was jammed too; they were standing tied in the walk way. I had a seat and officers were sitting with me. We had wonderful conversations when, suddenly, I had an urgent need to go to the bathroom. I tried to make my way through the packed train; there was no way to reach the bathroom. And so it came, diarrhea. I felt that by going back and sitting down I had a better chance to stop the mess. So I did and we started to talk again and it just kept coming. The officers looked at each other, thinking they let gas out, never thinking that it could be me, a pretty young lady.

When we rolled into the station Weimar, they offered to heave me out of the window -- no way could you get through the jammed aisle. Well, that did it. The mess ran down my legs -- I could have died. I didn't say thank you; I just walked away. I wanted to die. I never was so embarrassed in my whole life. I had to take another little train from Weimar to Saalborn, an hour ride. I went to the bathroom to clean myself, no soap, just toilet paper, which at this time was cut up newspaper. Well, it certainly didn't do a good job. The

Trudy after her confirmation at the Lutheran Church aged 15 March 1941

smell stuck with me and I stayed in the little train for an hour on the outside platform between train cars, which was allowed during the war. My sister was waiting at the train station and hugged me, then walked away screaming, "Whoo! Do you stink! What happened?" In the guesthouse, the sweet owners told me to give all the clothes to them for cleaning. That horrible incident is still fresh in my mind. My sister and I had a good weekend together and I was happy to see that she settled nice in her new place with nice friends around away from home.

Meanwhile in 1942, air raids and bombardment had escalated tremendously. When I returned from visiting with my sister we had many, many bad nights. Whenever the sirens droned, we dressed quickly and went down into the cellar. Many times it shook like an earthquake. When the sirens sounded the "all clear", we could go upstairs; the bombardment was over for the time being and then we looked where the red sky was, where the bombardment took place and where everything was burning. Many, many times the windows were broken from the presence of the explosions and dust was everywhere. We weren't able to get replacement fast, so often the broken windows were boarded with plywood or cardboard for days.

Since 1943 all schools in Berlin had been closed and all school children under 16 years of age were evacuated to the country. I was sixteen years old and had to stay in Berlin to enter my "Pflichtjahr" (duty year). All girls of this age had to go through a year of service, which in my case meant being with a family with two toddlers. The fathers were drafted into the military and the mothers were left alone without help. You could say that the sixteen year old girls were maids! It was no fun, but somewhat better than what the sixteen year old boys had to go through: training for the military.

Between not having enough sleep with all the bombarding most of the nights and having to take care of two little boys, plus lots of housework when they napped, I walked around like a zombie. I was chronically fatigued. Several times I fainted on the street when I took the two little ones out for a walk. Finally the mother could not let me go out anymore with the kids. I was very glad about this because the three year old boy was uncontrollable, threw himself on the sidewalk and screamed his head off, while people walked by and shook there heads. It was very embarrassing. Between that and the nights with the constant wakefulness, insecurity, and feeling of terror, plus the frightening sights of leveled buildings, mountains of rubble, and wounded civilians, it was all psychologically eroding. The mother and children finally left Berlin, taking me with them, to escape to Schwerin, Mecklenburg, where Mrs. Dube's parents lived in a beautiful, peaceful surrounding. What a relief it was to be able to sleep again without air raids. My parents were very relieved to know that I was safe there. However, my sister in Thueringen and I in Schwerin were always worrying about my parents left behind in such a dangerous environment.

Berlin was a beautiful sophisticated city.

Unter de Linden boulevard was the pride of Berlin with rows of trees, palaces, gardens and important buildings. An equestrian statue of Frederick the Great was on one end and at the other end a mile away was the Brandenburg Gate.

Statue of Frederick the Great with linden trees.

Brandenburg Gate

After the war, all was in ruins.

Hungry people raising vegetables after the war in the garden area of the ruined Dom Cathedral.

People going to work in spite of the devastation all around.

This was the Tiergarten the largest green space in Berlin with a wooded park and a rose garden. Trees were cut and burned to keep people warm during the last winter of the war.

Bahnhof "Zoo" train station after an air raid.

After I finished my Pflichtjahr I went back to Berlin. I was homesick being separated from my parents. I started to work as an apprentice to become a librarian in a publishing house. Twice a week we had business classes in an empty school building, and we had to take turns to stay overnight completely alone to watch the building. What in the world could we have saved as a young inexperienced girl if the bombs would have hit? This was another scary situation. No telephone, often no electricity, in a big building all by yourself. During air raids I would just sit in the huge empty basement and pray for survival. The saying was, "You won't hear the bomb that is going to kill you. If you heard the bombs whistling on their way down they were far enough way." The only time we got undisturbed sleep was when the weather was bad. In October of 1944 we had 23 days of rain. Thank God, not much bombardment. We were able to sleep undisturbed.

Bombardment went on heavier than ever and one day at school we had an alarm and went down to the basement. The noise was unbelievable. Everything shook. When the attack was over and I could get out, I did not know which way was home. All around me were piles of collapsed buildings with heavy dust and smoke. It was very difficult to breathe. I walked over many smoky things until I could orient myself enough to find my way home. There was no longer any public transportation.

When my parents saw me full of dust, (9/11 in

New York reminded me of that day), they couldn't thank God enough that I had survived. I told them that I must have walked over things with very expensive statues; I saw so many lying around. My parents told me later that they were people, who burned and shrank.

Wintertime got mighty cold. The ovens were heated with coals; we were not able to get enough coals and on top of it, we had the broken windows again and again. Half-burned timber from collapsed buildings sawed and chopped to firewood sized chunks helped us a little.

As a teenager, my parents kept me very busy with all kinds of activities, like piano lessons, Ruderverein (Rowing Club), swimming, and tennis. On Sundays, my girlfriends and I got dressed nicely and went downtown to the more fashionable areas of Berlin, like the famous boulevard Kurfürstendamm. We would sit in an outside café and drink juice or lemonade; coffee was very hard to get, very scarce.

It was fun to see the people walk by. After we were seated, some young officers did come and ask if they could join our table. We enjoyed our conversations and one of them, Herr Roggenbuck, asked me if he could see me the next Sunday. I told him to meet me at our street; we could take a walk through our park. When I came home and told my parents that I met an officer and that we would meet next Sunday, they insisted that I had to bring him to our home to meet him. They were beyond being protective.

I didn't like to do that -- I hardly knew him but I had no choice.

Next Sunday came. I went to the corner of our street to tell him that my parents insisted on meeting him. He didn't mind, so we went. Well, my parents got to like him very, very much. My mother, especially, because he came from the same area my mother grew up in, Königsberg, Ostpreußen, which now was in Polish hands. He had lost his parents when they occupied East Prussia. My mother felt so sorry for him, invited him for many nights for a meal and get-together. Many times, when he was invited, I told my parents I had to go to a girlfriend's house to do homework together. He was a nice person but I had the feeling that my mom had the desire to have him as a son-in-law. Yes, he did like me a lot; for me, he just was a nice guy.

Well, his time in Berlin was up; he was called into Russia to fight the war. He kept writing letters and my mother insisted that I answer them. Soldiers always wanted to receive letters being on the front fighting, so we kept in touch.

One day coming home from school I found my mother crying with a letter in her hand. Ernst Roggenbuck, the officer she liked so much, was injured in a fight in Russia and he lost one eye. Immediately she put a care-packet together with all kind of goodies and told me to go the next day to Würzburg, a six to eight hour train ride, to visit him. I was not thrilled about it at all, but had no choice. I never had seen Würzburg

Ernest Roggenbuck and myself at the Berlin Zoo in the beginning of our friendship before my mother's death.

before and when I went to the place of the address, I found that it was a convent. The entrance was a big ugly door with a metal door knob and a small window opening in the door. I knocked at the door knob; a while later the opening moved and a head came up asking what I wanted. What I wanted was to run away fast -- I thought I saw a ghost. It was a nun. I had never seen one in my life; it looked so scary to me. She guided me to Ernst Roggenbuck and he was so surprised and happy to see me. He told me that he would be transferred to German-occupied Denmark after his injury was healed. I stayed two hours with him, wished him the very best and took the next train home for a long, long ride in the middle of the night.

Every able-bodied man now was fighting in all the surrounding countries. Thank God, they couldn't take my dad; he was very much needed in Berlin to take care of the chaos caused by the steady bombardment of the city. He also had to pull in all the men who owned their individual stores to decide if they had to go to the "front ", (war), or if they could help in the police department. Many brought my dad chocolate, meat and other rare goodies to beg him to let them stay with the police rather than going into the fighting.

Because of the shortage of men, all women had to go to work to keep everything going on the home front. They had no choice as to where they were placed. Due to my dad's position in the police force, he had to draft the owner of a fine Delicatessen store off Kurfürstendamm, the very best area in Berlin. Yet he placed him into the police department rather than sending him off to become a soldier. In turn, my dad asked him to hire my mom as a manager for his store, which he did. He was very generous with her hours, very thankful for my dad that he could stay in the country.

If possible, my dad used to come home for the midday meal, which used to be the main meal in Germany. He never had much time, so my mom had it ready when he walked in. One night we had again heavy bombardment and I was not able to go to school. My mom asked me to put the potatoes on at 11:30; she felt she had to check the store where she was hired as a manager because the owner's wife was away. She had no idea if any streetcars would run, but she wanted to try. It was January 29, 1944.

She was always back on time for the three of us to have our meal. My dad arrived for a short break in his very hectic position as a police officer, but Mom was not there. We waited fifteen minutes and the doorbell rang. I opened the door; there was a policeman asking for my dad. I didn't give it much thought -- he often got calls; phones were not working. They talked in the living room and Dad came out snow-white telling me that Mom was buried under the collapsed house, where the store was. The policeman came to us with an ambulance for survivors. They told me to stay in the ambulance; I was sitting there for hours, numb. I could see that the whole area had been devastated and was in utter ruins. There seemed to be nothing left standing but chimneys. Finally, Dad came back. He was crying.

They had found a body in very bad shape, disfigured. My dad could only recognize my mother's body by a familiar scarf . They put her in the back of the ambulance and we were driven, with Mom, to the funeral home.

There existed a cemetery for all the war victims, but my dad bought a nice plot in a private cemetery. The funeral took place on February 2nd. Considering how large the circle of our family and friends was, the group that could make it was small. Dad's brothers were soldiers everywhere, their wives and children were somewhere in the countryside away from the city, telephones were not working, and mail was slow. My dad's birthday was January 31st and we were all alone. It was my dad's 45th birthday; my mom was 43 years old. She was loved by everyone, always helping, always happy, a loving, caring, wonderful wife and mom.

Now we had a big problem. How can we give this earthshaking news to my sister, twelve years old? It was bad enough that she was separated from us. My mom wrote her letters everyday, my dad and I once in a while. Now she wouldn't get Mom's letters. We couldn't go to her until after the funeral.

My dad wrote a letter to Mrs. Geyer, the owner of the guesthouse to let her know that Mom was killed and not to tell our Irmi until we arrive one day after the funeral. In the meantime, Dad wrote her daily letters

Place my mother was killed on Kurfurstendamm.

People cleared the rubble off the streets by hand.

that Mom couldn't write because she was ill and that he and I would come and visit her on February 3rd. Well,the funeral was over and we were on the way to Thüringen to bring her this terrible news. Thank God that she found in Mrs. Geyer and the two daughters in Irmi's age a second family while she had to stay away from us. But after getting this shocking news she insisted to come home with us. This was not allowed; schools were closed. My dad promised her to move me also to Mrs. Geyer's place. Irmi was desperately in need of her own family. I didn't want to leave my dad behind with all the bombardment going on. On the other hand, my little sister needed me badly. So, I moved to Saalborn, Thüringen and had to take a job in Weimar in an office where help was desperately needed as there were no men around anywhere.

From the little village of Saalborn to Weimar we had an hour train ride; the train stopped at every little village and I had to get up at five a.m. to catch the train by six a.m., the only one in the morning running. From the guesthouse up the mountain to the train was a twenty minute walk in the ice and snow. The guesthouse had an outhouse; the owner had to get up before me in order to warm the oven with wood and coal to heat the big kitchen and serve some tea or milk, or make me breakfast and lunch. Her husband and both sons were in the war, she and her two daughters had their hands full taking care of all of the animals -- cows, pigs, geese, chickens, and rabbits -- and attending to the grain fields. They made their own butter. Bread and homemade cake was always fresh. Breakfast was a huge selection of delicious cakes during the week. Weekends were a splurge of eggs, bacon, ham, and home-fried potatoes -- a big treat for us city folks, where food was very much rationed. On Sundays, they killed a rabbit or chicken or goose. I made sure to be far enough away not to see it.

My little sister loved the primitive country living with the outhouse and the whole works. I hated it all, but the loving care of Mrs. Geyer and having my sister with me and the two daughters befriending me made it easier. My sister enjoyed helping to feed the animals and on weekends I helped going out with the daughters working in the fields. Dear old Grandma, Mrs. Geyer's mother, had died and later we received the notice that one son was killed in the war.

Whenever Irmi and I heard on the radio that Berlin was heavily bombed again, we worried so much about our dad. He did write to us daily in order to keep us calm. At least he could relax, knowing that we were safe.

After having been there with my sister for about half of a year and having seen that she adjusted nicely with all the friends she made in the country surrounding, I begged my father to please let me come home again. I hated the primitive life, with the outhouse, etc. and missed my friends very much. One day our dad wrote a letter to us to let us know that he thought it would be best to have a woman in the house to take care of us and he was thinking about getting married again because in his job he was away from home most of the time and I, as a teenager, shouldn't be left alone. Also, when the war was over and Irmi would come home, we would definitely need a woman in the

The beautiful little village SAALBORN BEI' WEIMAR where my sister Irmi' had to stay after evacuation from Berlin. I did join her for 6 months after Mom was killed in Berlin.

house. He said that no one could replace our beloved Mom, but he felt close to the lady who was taking care of our home, so he has a warm meal and a clean place when he came home for a little break. That letter hit the ceiling. "Another woman dares to take our mom's place? " We were so very upset and I told him in my letter that I can handle the household and do the cooking; I was old enough. No, our dad had made up his mind; he wanted us to meet this woman at her hometown in Breslau, where all her family lived. We wrote him that we didn't want to go to Breslau to meet her but Dad picked us up and we had no choice. With hate in our hearts we went to Breslau, giving our poor dad a hard time and at the gathering we were very rude to the whole family. I guess my dad was very embarrassed having two very badly behaved daughters.

My dad got married quietly before I was allowed to come home to Berlin. With my dad gone most of the time, I gave the new wife a very hard time, although she tried so hard to keep everything peaceful for my dad's sake. I just felt so hurt that she, as a stranger, took our mom's position.

Before and during that time, I did get a lot of letters from Ernst Roggenbuck. I wrote him how unhappy I was. He came back with the offer to marry me, take me out of Berlin before the Russians would arrive and take me to Denmark, where he was now stationed. It was so tempting to escape the bombardment, the Russians arrival sooner or later, and the tensions in our home. I wrote back that I would love to join him, but to let him know that I respect him a lot but cannot feel any love towards him. That is all he had to hear. He said that the love would eventually develop when we lived together and I said YES. He got in touch with my dad and Dad agreed. I guess he was happy to get me out of there, especially for safety reasons.

A lot of paperwork started rolling in. When an officer planned to get married, the woman had to give evidence that she was "Aryan", that only German blood was in her veins. My father had to prepare a family tree of several generations back. in order to prove that

everything was okay. I was cleared to marry an officer. We sat April 11, 1945, my dad and Lina, his wife, prepared for the wedding. The Russians were already close to us -- we could not get much food or anything else. I borrowed a wedding dress from our neighbor; we made arrangements for a church wedding and we could still order a horse and carriage to bring us to church.

As I mentioned before, not many relatives were around anymore, but we had about three weeks to contact them and around twenty of them were able to come. My sister was not among them; Berlin was already surrounded by the Russians.

My future husband and two of his soldiers arrived the night before by plane from Denmark with all the most wonderful food I could imagine and, on top of that, red roses. We got married the next day in the church where I was confirmed. We were called three times up and down to the cellar by the air raid sirens during the ceremony. My dad had us all back to his home for a celebration with all the food my husband had brought from Denmark. In spite of the bombardment all of us were dancing and singing and celebrating. My uncle noticed there was blood on the floor. It was my time of month and I had begun to hemorrhage. Due to the bombardment, there was no transportation for our guests to get home. The girls stayed in one room and the men stayed in another. No wedding night.

My husband had the airline tickets for the next day to get me out; there was no way that I was able to do it because of my condition. I had to stay in bed and say goodbye. My husband was scared stiff to leave me behind with the Russians so very close to Berlin. Here I was, married for the reason to get out of hell and now I was stuck. A few days later I was fine again. We could hear the Russians all around, shooting, getting closer and closer. One day, when my dad came home for a short time for the midday meal, two soldiers stood on our door and begged to get civilian clothes before the Russians came and killed them. My poor father didn't know what to do. If the Nazis would find out, he would be killed; otherwise, the Russians would kill the soldiers. We were surrounded -- no more getting out. He gave them civilian clothes and asked them to bury their uniforms deep, away from our home. We wished them good luck; never heard from them again because Russians were suspicious seeing two young men in civilian clothes. We could just hope that they were able to make it home to their families.

The Russians now were fighting in our neighborhood. A horse was killed in front of our house. We had nothing to eat anymore and we could see old men and crippled soldiers going at it with their knives to cut meat for a meal. My stepmother brought a piece, too; it tasted so good, a piece of meat cooked in water.

There was no more mail coming in or out so we didn't know how my sister was or vice versa. We were cut off from the world, except for radio, where Hitler still told us to fight, not to give up. Whenever shooting took place, we were in the cellar. One day after it got quiet and we came up, one dead Russian was lying in front of the house. Oh my god -- if the Russians came through and saw that, we all would be killed. They might think it was us, so the neighbors got together fast and buried him in the green strip on our street. A few days later we had several German soldiers lying dead on the street; they all had to be buried in the neighborhood. Well, the Russians finally conquered; the war was over, the bombardment stopped, but the horror did not.. The Russians were there. There was wide spread looting, raping and murder, underpinned by a grotesque element of sadism. Women and children were raped, tortured and mutilated. There bruised and battered corpses were left in the road.

My dad gave me strict instructions not to go out and if the Russians would come in, to have a cane, put a kerchief on close to my face and limp bent over like an old woman. If they would find me, to say "Machine kaputt; " I don't know where that came from, but my dad in his police barracks heard a lot about what was going on. For instance, the Russians went from house to house and collected all of the gold. If you couldn't get your rings off, they just cut fingers off. Many people had gold fillings in their teeth -- they were chopped off. After the Russians now had conquered all of Berlin, the news came through that the French, English, and American troops would get a piece of Berlin, divided into four sections. We heard that our section would be British; that was good news, but in the meantime, the Russians wanted to take out to Russia anything left in factories. So they picked us up by trucks from house to house, everybody who was able to move from sixteen years of age to eighty. They drove us to factories and we had a tough time carrying huge equipment and loading it into the waiting trucks. They were long, long days; at noon we became a bowl of watery soup. If you were not able to carry heavy loads, you got hit badly or sometimes shot. They were in a hurry to get out as much as they could before the British would come. In the short lunch time, one could see Russian soldiers picking out the women; they all were raped. One officer waved me over and I went over to him, scared. He took me into his office, sat me down and told me to help him translate. He had found out that I had six years of English, thanks to my parents sending me to a private school. He spoke in broken German but no English and needed to meet the British officers to organize with them the process of the departure of the Russian troops of what would become the British sector of Berlin, and to decide among all the allies on the borders which would divide Berlin into four sectors. He drove me with his jeep to meet the British and behaved like a true gentleman towards me, apologizing for the Russian soldiers being so cruel. What a great relief it was -- I was truly blessed.

Shortly afterwards we heard on the radio that the Russians were to leave our section and on the next day the British would take over. Before that happened, the Russians took my dad from his job and gone he was. No one had any idea why, how, or where. We just could pray they would bring him back to us.

When the British soldiers, on their trucks with guns in hand, moved into our section, we survivors were standing on the streets waving and welcoming them. They were baffled: here they were, the enemies, who had destroyed our cities and killed millions with their bombs, getting a big happy welcome from us. They had no idea what we had gone through with the Russians.

Things slowly got better -- no more fear to go out in the street, schools started to open again, and my poor little sister came home, but Dad was still missing. To support our family I worked at WMF as a salesgirl. Dad's wife also worked, but I don't know at what. Food was still rare. When they opened a butcher shop with horse meat, I stayed in line with the neighbors for hours to get a little meat.

I visited my mom's grave a lot. We had a bench next to her grave and I sat there for hours praying for my dad to come home. One day my sister and I went on our bicycles to the cemetery, sat on the bench, and talked about good old times. We heard a horse and carriage in the distance, which was not unusual. The funerals were done with a horse and carriage, not having any trucks or cars left. The closer they came, the more we smelled something very rotten. It was unbearable when they passed by and we were shocked to no end to see dead bodies, one on top of the other heaped up to a mountain. We left in terrible shock. It was the time when the Germans were ordered to dig out the bodies which were buried everywhere on the streets during the last fight between the Russians and the Germans. For a long time, my sister and I would not enter the cemetery anymore.

One afternoon my sister and I were home alone -- our stepmother was working -- when the door bell ran. I opened the door and saw my dad thin as a skeleton; I hardly recognized him. He had lost so much weight and his smile was gone -- an old shaky man. We were so happy to have him back and he told us that the Russians wanted to get some names out of him and tortured him to no end, put a pistol to his chest many times. He didn't know what they were talking about and they finally recognized that they had the wrong man and let him go.

I had not heard anything from my husband; he was a POW in Denmark.

The time came for West Germany and West Berlin to change the currency (Currency Reform of 6-21-1948) from Reichsmark to Deutsche Mark. Our old money was invalid the next day and all of us got sixty D-mark to start with, until we could change our old money to our new currency. Now we all had to work to make money. Sixty mark didn't last long. I started as a shorthand teacher in a school for grown-ups. I had no degree but they were wiling to take me for the time being; they didn't have enough help. Young men and women needed business education to get into a job market. They all missed out the last years of war without training; I taught stenography and math.

With earning my own money, I decided to move out of my father's home because of the tension with my stepmother. I was still rebelling with my sister and now that I was married, my dad would not hold me back any longer. I rented a room in a couple's home. It was not easy, so young and so alone, but I managed.

Then, my husband came back home to me, still a virgin, after being married for half a year. We had to get to know each other. He tried to get us larger living quarters, however that was very hard because the city lay in ruins.

All the people who had left their apartments and houses during the war and didn't come back right away had to rent the space through the owner of the apartments. Often, the rental agents had no idea how to contact these scattered owners nor whether they even survived the war, yet they had the authority from the state to rent them out. Once it was rented, the owners couldn't come back to get them out. These were all furnished apartments or houses left behind when the owners had fled the city to escape the air attacks.

We finally were able to get a completely furnished apartment in a nice area, which cost my husband a lot of maneuvering. Now I felt good to be married; someone took care of me in a very caring way. He was a kind, loving man. A few of his POW buddies went to school to study law and I told him he should go ahead to do the same with them. He wouldn't hear of it; his wife had to quit working, stay home and have children. All these German men at this time wanted to be the only bread-winners for their family, including my dad. My husband got a job as a salesman and I got pregnant.

Food was very scarce. We had an aunt in the DDR (Deutsche Demokratische Republik), the Soviet controlled zone of Germany. She had a huge garden and invited me to visit whenever I wanted. While my husband was at work, I hopped on the very overcrowded train and got to her place within an hour. Very pregnant, I often had to hang on the outside platform or steps of a train from Berlin-Spandau to Finkenkrug. In my aunt's garden, there was all the fruit on the trees and the berries and the vegetables I could eat and take home goodies to my husband. I never told him how dangerous the ride was, hanging outside; he wouldn't have let me go.

The trains were so overcrowded because we in the city needed to get into the farmland around Berlin to bargain for food. Not everyone had relatives to fall back on as we did. Many people brought silverware, oriental pieces, jewelry, etc. to the farmers in the DDR to trade for potatoes and vegetables. Some farmers close to Berlin got rich by taking advantage of our situation.

However, soon after that my aunt, our main source for food, passed away. We as newly weds did not have silverware or china to trade . My parents had given me a hope chest with all kinds of goodies. They had taken it to friends in the outskirts of Berlin to have it safe from bombardment. It so happened that their house was completely destroyed, even that far away from the city. So my silverware and china from my hope chest was gone. My mother's and my own jewelry had all been taken away from us when the Russians occupied our city. Nothing to bargain for food.

As usual, I prepared dinner for my husband and, whoops!, contractions set in. I finished cooking the food, which were wild mushrooms and potatoes. I looked out of the window, waiting for my husband. When he arrived, I told him that I had contractions. At that time, you didn't go to the doctor for check-ups and didn't get any instructions for what to do. My husband wanted to go with me to the clinic right away. I was very calm and told him that wc can cat in peace and then walk to the clinic, ten blocks away. So we did. My husband had to be in the waiting room for hours. Finally, and with lots of pain, my little baby girl came into the world. I had a private room and I could keep the baby as long as I wanted to. My husband also could stay with me. We were a happy little family. After seven days, I came home with our Karin.

My sister visited us a lot, complaining about the life she had with my stepmother. She wanted to move to us very badly but of course my dad wouldn't allow it. My husband's little brother found us one day. He was a refugee and orphan from Danzig, the Baltic city, which was formerly part of Germany but since the end of the war had become part of Poland and was called Gdansk. He was fifteen years old when he came to stay with us, so my family Roggenbuck was growing.

My dad's police station was right across from us, so he came to see us often. He was reinstated in his old position, a top officer, after the Nazis had demoted him. We had a good relationship also with his wife. I guess I had grown up, being married and a mother, and understood that Dad was too young stay single. He was only fifty years old and needed a companion.

Taking care of a baby at that time was very difficult. We had no soap, no diapers, and not enough wood or coal to heat the stove. In January 1947 the temperature dropped to 18 degrees below 0 (Fahrenheit!). Some people were burning up their last of furniture to stay warm. I had to cut bed linens into pieces for diapers, had to wash them in clear water and hang them as close to the stove as possible to dry. In order to have a warm room, we had to go through the woods to gather kindling. In those days we were allowed to cut trees, but they were all wet and let the fire go out. My poor baby had lots of rashes; there was no cream or medicine available to heal it fast. Thank God I was able to give Karin mother's milk; since other milk was also very hard to come by.

Karin 1946

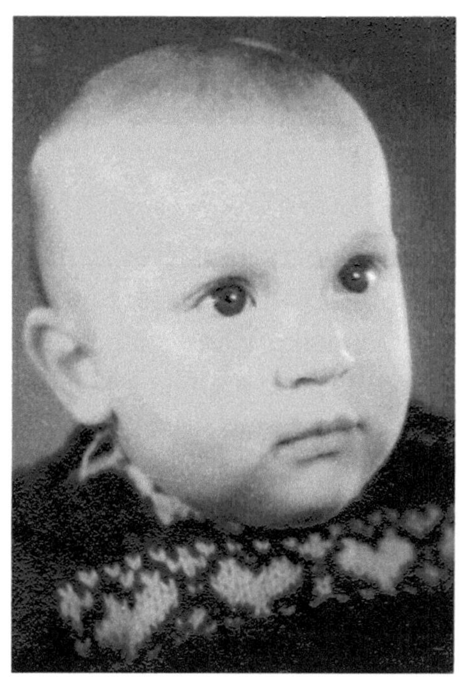

Trudchen and Karin
1947

Karin was one year old and had never seen a piece of chocolate. There was a black market in the area where British soldiers wanted to trade their chocolate and cigarettes for other things. These items were very valuable.

One evening I went to the black market to see what the British soldiers were looking for. A soldier approached me and asked for a "Knirps" (a collapsible umbrella with a cover). That was a pretty neat thing to have. I had one, it was ripped and no cover. I asked him how much chocolate he would give for "a beautiful new Knirps". I was happy with his answer and told him to meet me the next evening at a certain time. I went home, had a piece of fine soft leather, fixed it for a cover for the ripped umbrella. It did look rich and beautiful. Off I went the next evening with my heart pounding. What would happen if he would open the umbrella? But I had to give it a try to give my baby a treat. I handed him the umbrella, he did like what he saw, a beautiful leather cover, and he asked if the umbrella worked. I said, "Of course! It is brand new. Would you like me to open it?" knowing that he had to be very careful not to be caught. The black market was a definite no-no to either party. He trusted me, gave me the chocolate, and I went home not hurrying too much to not let him get suspicious. I felt like a bad criminal. But it was surpassed by the joy to introduce my sweet Karin to a better taste in life.

My husband's surviving relatives were from Danzig, now part of Poland. They settled on the Baltic

Sea as fishermen. They caught a lot of flounders and smoked them. Knowing that we city folk had nothing to eat, they asked us to come and pick some up. Not being allowed to go to the East Zone we had to hire a guide whose business it was to get us over the border in the middle of the night into the Russian Zone. A lot of walking in the dark was involved, for hours, and prayers that the Russians would not check our pass ports in the train once we had entered the Russian Zone illegally. We arrived with empty suitcases and filled them up with smoked delicious flounders, a real delicacy. Trains ran very infrequently. I remember lying on the cold floor with my husband and many other passengers in the waiting room at a train station in the middle of the night, hoping for a train to come to take us back to the place where we got the guide to walk us back to West Berlin. What we did not realize was that the smell of the fresh smoked fish was so strong that it was noticed. We just prayed that no Russian soldier would come near us. You certainly were not allowed to take anything out of the Russian occupied part of Germany, or for that matter be in it unless you lived there. Thank God, we made it home safely, but I had nightmares for years thereafter and we never would do it again. All this just to get something to eat. Now we were able to trade with the farmers for other food items, and also enjoy some of the delicious smoked flounder ourselves.

When I remember those days today even I find it hard to believe that there actually was a time when we would eat cheese (Harzer Kaese) that had spoiled and was filled with little white creatures with black heads. It was either eat that or have nothing. When there was food available, we ate what there was. At that time anything edible was precious and could not be wasted.

My poor Karin got the whooping coughs and it took a long time to get rid of them, coughing constantly day and night. The very few doctors we had didn't have time to see us; it was so scary. Through all that, Karin developed nicely and didn't finish my milk in the end. I had no instruction of what to do and ended up with a bad infection. They got me and Karin to the hospital; I needed surgery to drain the infection. My husband got me a private room and I could keep my baby with me. Before the surgery, the surgeon came and introduced himself and examined me. What a good looking, charming guy he was. During the surgery I woke up and was beyond myself with fear, seeing the doctors and nurses with their masks over me, handling knives. I screamed "Scheiße! " (shit!) and was put to sleep again. The next day the surgeon came into my room to check if I remembered waking up.

"Do you recall saying something during the surgery? " he asked. "You bet I did. I screamed "Scheiße," I answered. Dr. Klawitter burst out laughing and said, "I can't believe such a word coming out of such a pretty lady's mouth."

Well, I had to stay in the hospital for ten days. Dr. Klawitter visited me every evening and we got to know each other very well. He was a widower and we fell in love with each other. Now I knew what love was. When I was released from the hospital, we agreed not to pursue it any further. I had a good husband and a wonderful little girl. It was a heartbreaking good-bye. I was not the same person at home anymore. My thoughts were a lot with my first love, dreaming all the time.

One day we met by coincidence in a shopping area, spent some time together and I promised Dr. Klawitter that I would ask my husband for a divorce. My Karin was one year old and just took her first steps between Dad and Mom, a big event for us.

I hesitated to approach my husband; he didn't deserve to get hurt, but one night I told him and needless to say, he was outraged. He went to my dad and asked him to talk sense into me. So my father came to visit me and let me know how disappointed he was in the way I behaved. I reminded him and my husband that I had honestly told Ernst Roggenbuck that I did not love him but was tempted to marry him to get out of Berlin before the Russians arrived. But now I had a child. My feelings were so strong towards gaining a future marriage with lots of love, that no one could talk me out of it.

Dr. Klawitter approached my father and my husband to marry me and promised that he would take good care of my daughter. It was a big fight and a big court hearing, but in the end I got my divorce because one time I provoked my husband and he lost control and hit me. I didn't ask for child support; Dr. Klawitter took care of us.

Trudy and her second husband Dr. Klawitter.

I was in no rush to get married again right away; I had to get to know the doctor a little more. Rushing into marriage once for the wrong reasons was enough warning for me not to do it again. We did live together for a year; he still had his apartment in the hospital. As a gynecologist, he was called out many nights to deliver a baby, so the hospital apartment came in handy. He was most anxious to marry as soon as possible because he had a son from his deceased wife who lived in Vienna with his aunts until my future husband could give him a home. So, we settled the date on my birthday in June. My dad in the meantime settled down, got to know my future husband, respected him, and planned to have our wedding in his home with relatives and friends. My dad and my future husband's sister and brother-in-law were supposed to meet us at the courthouse for a short wedding and then all go to my father's home for a celebration with the rest of the guests.

That morning my future husband acted very strange. He hardly talked when we went to the courthouse. I had never seen him this way. When I asked him what the matter was, he didn't answer. We had no arguments before; I didn't know what to make of it. Well, we got to the courthouse, got the papers signed and my new husband turned to my father and told him he had something to do in the hospital; he would later come to the house. That didn't sound right, so we went to my dad's house and all the guests were there to congratulate us and celebrate the wedding. I told everybody that my husband would come a little later. Hours and hours passed away, no husband in sight. At this time no one had telephones, so we couldn't contact him. The time came that the guests left and Dad asked me to stay with my little Karin in his house. He was afraid to leave me alone under these circumstances. There went another wedding night without a husband. The next morning, my dad went to the hospital to find out what was going on. My husband told him that he wrote a poem to his deceased wife apologizing to her for getting married again, even though he had promised her on her death bed that he would only live for their son, Klaus, and never get married again. His conscience was bothering him. He had studied medicine in Vienna and met a beautiful girl there; they had an affair. He was then drafted into the Air Force during the war and shipped, as a doctor, to Paris, France. He had had a wonderful time there; of course, I never heard details. One day he had received a letter that his girl in Vienna was pregnant. He had not planned to marry her. The little boy was born; his father had not able to see him while in combat in France. Later on he had received a letter from his girlfriend's sister informing him that she was dying from brain cancer. At that time he had been able to leave France and fly to Vienna to see her. After he had seen his son, he had married his girlfriend for his son's sake. He had felt so guilty that he had promised her on her death bed to take good care of their son and never to get married again. Then he had to leave his son behind with his wife's sister and fly back to France.

These details were never told to me before the marriage. So my second marriage didn't start off too well. I was deeply hurt. This was my second wedding without a wedding night -- oh, well.

My husband moved into my apartment. He went to Vienna to pick up his son Klaus. Klaus was a small, adorable little boy, four years of age; I couldn't help loving him right away. He loved my little girl Karin and vice versa. With two lovely children from his and my former marriage, I was still longing for a third child from my husband. He refused. The guilt complex toward his former wife and his promise on her death bed just to live for their son was deep in him. He enlarged photographs of his former wife and placed them on the walls so Klaus could see his mother. That was understandable since Klaus did not know his mother, but it did hurt me a lot. Whenever my husband brought home some extra food from the hospital he gave it only to Klaus. This favoritism he continued to show through the coming years. It was not the ideal marriage after all.

He was an excellent doctor and in his free time read a lot of medical books. He could never get enough medical knowledge. Besides vacation time, I felt very much alone with my two children, but I made the best of it. We were surrounded by lakes and woods, so I took my children swimming, skiing, ice-skating, bicycling, etc. Other neighbors' kids came along; they always enjoyed being with us. It was always a happy gathering. Besides, I had plenty of relatives and certainly kept busy with everybody, except the ones living in the Russian sector. We were never allowed to visit them.

The time came for West Germany and West Berlin to change the currency (Currency Reform of 6-21-1948) from Reichsmark to Deutsche Mark. Our old money was invalid the next day and all of us got sixty D-mark to start with. Immediately afterwards, the alliance between West and East had broken down. The conflict had led to disputes over access roads into Berlin, the final break between West and East. Food had already been scarce. It got almost non-existent when the Soviets blocked all access by land to Berlin: roads, rails, boats. We became an "island in the Red Sea". West Berlin only survived through the Air Lift, an incredible endeavor of the Western Allies. For almost 18 months the needs of the former German capitol were met thru the largest airlift in history. They supplied a city of 2.4 million west Berlinners with coal, medical and food supplies. By May of 1949 the Soviets admitted failure and re-opened road and rail service to West Berlin.

My dad's second wife became pregnant and they got a beautiful little girl, my stepsister. She is younger than my daughter Karin. They enjoyed growing up together with Klaus. Dad smoked a lot and came down with lung cancer. He had to suffer something terrible because the pain medication was still rare; being surrounded by the Russians, everything had to be flown in. He begged my husband as the doctor to let him die, to give him something to let go. Of course, my husband couldn't do it. I still have a guilt complex about one thing. Before my husband and I went to a concert in the afternoon, we visited my dad in the hospital. I asked what he would like to have and he said an orange, which was very hard to get. He was already in a dying stage. Instead of canceling the concert, I felt I should have searched in stores for an orange and brought it to him. I was selfish, and he died that evening.

He passed away when his little sweetheart daughter Christel was four years old. It was an unforgettable funeral.

We buried Dad next to my mom. All the police were there, by the hundreds, when we arrived to form an honor guard to show their last respect to my dad. He was well known and well liked by everyone.

We kept in touch with my stepmother and

Christel, my half sister. My sister Irmi was in college, so she had moved out of my father's home. She was still so bitter towards our stepmother that she and my father's wife didn't have much contact through the years. Later in life, I realized that my father's wife Lina was a very good woman who took wonderful care of my dad through all his illness and pain. After I grew up I understood better why my father married so fast after my mother's death. He needed someone to take care of my sister and myself, while he was working hard at all hours as the police chief.

My husband and I enjoyed traveling with the children on his vacation. It was always difficult for us in West Berlin to get a transit visa once a year from the East German authorities to allow us to travel from West Berlin through the Russian-occupied East Germany into the West German Zone. They made it very difficult. We felt we lived on an island surrounded by Russians.

We planned one summer vacation to climb the Alps in Italy, so we planned to send the children to Vienna, Austria, by plane from Munich to our relatives. We got the passports from the Russians for one trip per year and off we went from West Berlin through the Russian-occupied East Zone to West Germany. No one ever was allowed to get off the Autobahn on any exit until you reached the check-point. There you usually had to stay in line for hours to show your passport and get all your possessions checked in the car. We had bought airline tickets for the children to put them into the plane for Vienna and we got nervous standing in line to get the permission to drive to the West of

My father Erich Jagode with Karin, Cristel and Klaus Klawitter, my stepson, about 1949

Cemeteries in Germany are always beautiful park settings with fresh flowers. This is a photo of my parent's graves.

Karin with her
Schultuete the first
day of school
1952

Christel,
Karin's aunt, 2
years younger than
Karin
with her Schultuete
1954

My sister Irmi and niece Kirsten

1954

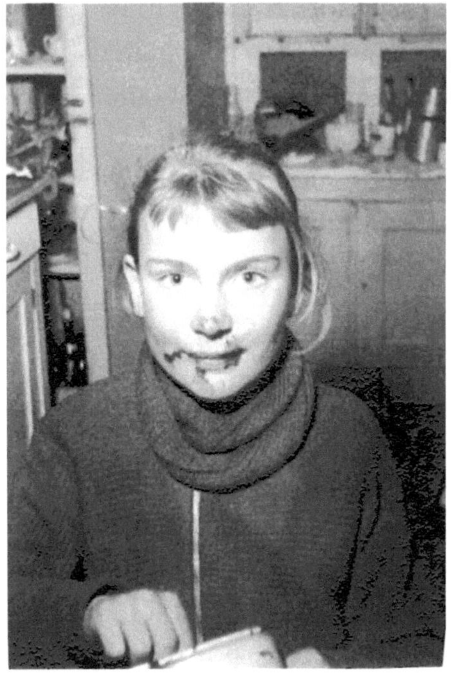

Karin and Karin

with Lina, my stepmother
during our painful
separation

1955

Germany. Time was getting close to catch the plane. The border control took the passports from us, let my husband and children go and told me I had to go back to Berlin, four hour ride on the Autobahn). The reason? The official stamp was next to my pass photo, not on it. My husband argued that it was their fault, putting the stamp next to the picture but they didn't care. My husband told me that he could take the kids to the airport and then go to an official place in West Germany to get a stamp on the picture. So there I was, without a passport, my family leaving. There was nothing to sit down on, nothing to eat or drink, a primitive border check point. I walked up and down forever; it got dark and a Russian soldier with his gun noticed me and asked for a passport. I explained to him through an East German police guy that my husband took the passport to get a stamp. "No passport -- jail. "

Yes, I ended up in a filthy cell and thought that I may end up in Siberia. Every so often the Russians peeked in through a little window with bars. The time seemed endless in jail. It happened on a weekend and all the official offices were closed. Nothing could be done until Monday. But even then I was not sure the Russians would accept a stamp on their passport from the West. It was an endless waiting and my fantasy went wild. A Russian soldier came in finally and handed me my passport. It was too good to be true. My husband could not come back to the Russian zone himself; he would have lost his one time permission to go to the West Zone, so he asked a truck driver to bring me the corrected passport and it worked. I was let go. I had to walk through the no-man's -land between the East and West checkpoints and into the West to be reunited with my husband again. That experience put a damper on our trip.

My husband worked full time in a hospital in West Berlin, but also three evenings a week in a clinic in Falkensee, which was a suburb of West Berlin, but now in the Russian zone. He got a pass to take the train from West Berlin to the clinic in the East, because they needed doctors badly; lots of them had escaped to the West. He received his salary from East Germany in a different currency than that from West Berlin. An east mark was only worth one fourth of a West mark. In order not to lose three fourth of his salary's worth, I had to spend the money in the East Even though there truly was not much to shop for, I had to go shopping in East Berlin. Of course, in order to go to East Berlin, they had to give me a pass for shopping.

My husband continued the clinic visits, feeling sorry for all the poor patients. Doctors in East Germany became more and more rare as lots of them escaped to West Germany. Many times they offered my husband a very well-paid position to bring his family over to live in East Germany. Of course we would not do that no matter how much they offered. The border controls between East and West became tighter and tighter as time went on. They started to bodily check us coming out of East Germany or East Berlin after shopping or visiting relatives. Under these conditions my husband felt it was no longer safe and he had to quit his position in East Germany.

West Berlin, where we lived, was one little island surrounded by the Russians. We could not go far at all. When we went out with our sailboat on the beautiful Wannsee and other lovely lakes in Berlin, we had to make sure that the wind would not drift us into the Russian zone. You could see the guards watching on the shores, ready to catch the Westerners. The lakes in West Berlin were filled with expensive boats while the other side was absolutely empty. There was no money for luxury.

My husband continued to work in the hospital in West Berlin and got on the waiting list for opening his own practice in the area. There was a two year waiting period because of overcrowded conditions in West Berlin; many doctors and lawyers who had chosen exile because of Nazi persecution had returned to Berlin and were given preference due to the restitution law (Wiedergutmachungsabkommen between Adenauer and Israel of 1952 became effective in1953).

My husband decided to go to America for one year as an exchange doctor to see what was new in his field of medicine. It was a very difficult decision to leave us behind. I brought him to the ship to say good-bye for a whole year. That was the year of 1957. We sent letters back and forth. He would tell us of his new experiences in the USA. One day he went to Time Square, dressed in his Lederhosen. People stopped him, invited him for dinner to get to know more about German traditions. He worked in a big hospital in

Klaus, me and Karin mid 1950's

Irmi im Olympiastadion 1951

Irmi in Olympic stadium in 1951 during her college years

Lake Vacation in Maine 1950's Klaus, me, Gerd, and Karin

Brooklyn and was very blessed. The gardener and his wife were refugees from Estonia. The wife used to be the secretary of the former president of Estonia. They were very sweet people who had my husband over in their home next to the hospital quite often for special dinners. I was happy that someone nice took care of him. He also joined a group of cello players. They were doctors from several hospitals who got together every so often for concerts. That was one of his hobbies, classical music. In the meantime life went on in Berlin without my husband at my side. In the summer my husband sent us for six weeks to a beautiful beach on the Baltic Sea for vacation. I am not kidding, it rained all the time and the weather insurance returned all the money to us.

Thank God, I had a lot of relatives and friends at home. My sister and her wonderful fiancé Horst visited me a lot; and Karin and Klaus kept me busy too. Christel, my half sister, a year younger than Karin, was also a joy to be with; the kids were great friends and good playmates.

One afternoon, I took my two children shopping on Kurfürstendamm, the famous boulevard in West Berlin. Afterwards we had ice cream and cake in the outside café at the Hotel Kempinsky, a five star hotel. We talked about their dad in America and how much we missed being with him. Suddenly a handsome man came up to our table, introduced himself and told me that he overheard our conversation. He had his own business in Germany and America, flying back and forth. He had a new device in his hotel room at the Kempinsky and would like for us to come up and talk to our dad into the tape recorder. He was going to fly back the next day and call my husband to invite him to his home in New York.

We went up to his room and talked to my husband. At this time telephone calls were a no-no, much, much too expensive and on top of that, my husband had no income for a year as an exchange doctor. So, we thanked our new friend and went home very excited. My husband wrote us a letter that Mr. X had called him and he had gone to his beautiful mansion for dinner and heard our voices. Mr. X and his wife also invited his German secretary with her husband, the Hollanders. They became very close friends with my husband, took him to the beach every weekend and to their home. I was very relieved that he had made some more friends.

He sent us pictures of his new friends and we also heard from Mr. X again, when he returned to Berlin on a business trip, bringing us a tape from my husband. After traveling around in his spare time with his new friends, he got to like the idea of being able to move about freely without the restricting borders set by the Russians in Berlin. We wrote back and forth and it sounded quite inviting, settling in the good USA, but it was not that easy. My husband would have to come back to get an Immigration Visa; since doctors were scarce in the USA in those days, that would not be a problem. However, once he got that Visa, he would have to take an internship again for two years. At that time, he would receive just a very minimum paycheck. That meant I had to work. As a German citizen, you only could work if you had a sponsor. Well, Mr. X offered to sponsor me to come to this country.

In the meantime my husband got introduced to the German director of Church World Service. They needed translators and with my six years of English in school I fit right in. Our biggest concern of course was what we would do with our children. With both of us working, who would take care of them? My sister and her husband offered to take my Karin, who was only eight years old, if they could move into our apartment. Living spaces were very hard to get after the war with all of the bombardment -- lots and lots of ruins around. Horst, my sister's husband, still went to college, so my sister gave up her college education in order to make money. She was also pregnant, so my Karin was pretty much on her own too in Berlin, but at least she had her friends and schoolmates, plus some relatives around her. Her father hardly ever visited her. He also did not contribute any money. In order to get the divorce, we told him that he didn't have to pay alimony. It would have been nice to bring her some gifts or take her out once in a while, but no. He did come for her birthday after being reminded by my sister. Thank God that Horst was home a lot with his studies -- Karin loved him so much. He was very good to her; so was my sister, though she had very little time because of her work. My stepmother was kind too, to take my Karin to her house ever so often, and my little sister Christel and Karin became good friends and playmates.

Klaus went back to Vienna to his late mother's sister to stay with her for a year until my husband and I found a place to live and I got acquainted with my job, never having worked before in our marriage. Also, we had to see how my husband's immigration worked out; assuming he would have to go back to Germany eventually for his visa and green card in order be able to work in the United States.

Here I was, waiting in Berlin for my visa to leave my children behind and to join my husband. I was so torn apart. Every day the mail came, my heart pounded heavily -- was this the day for the visa to arrive? It took about two to three months and there it was; lots of tears were running. I had to bring Klaus to the airport for Vienna; it was also very hard to separate Karin and Klaus, growing up together. My sister and brother-in-law moved in and everybody brought me to the train station to wave good-bye to me. Oh, God, I still see my Karin crying while the train rolled away; she was embraced by my sister and brother-in-law. Writing it now, I am crying again. It was an unforgettable good-bye, that little eight-year-old girl.

I promised my kids that we would be united within a year. I boarded my ship , the "BERLIN ," in Bremen and crossed the ocean with lots of sadness but also with excitement to see my husband again. It was a long trip with lots of seasickness, not very pleasant. When we finally arrived in New York and saw, the Statue of Liberty greeting us and the Manhattan skyline with all the skyscrapers, I knew I was entering a new world.

And there was my husband, on the pier, waving at me. It felt so good to have him hold me in his arms -- I felt protected again. He drove me to Brooklyn to his hospital. Along the roads I saw people's clothes hanging out of the windows and the dirt on the streets

That was a big shocker for me, a big downer to see the clothes hanging out of the window. In Berlin the laundry hung in a private garden or we used dryers.

The Estonian couple, Mr. and Mrs. Meikup, the gardener for the hospital and his wife, who had befriended my husband earlier, had invited me to stay with them while he finished his year of doctoral exchange visit. I gratefully accepted their invitation. Upon arrival, they gave me a wonderful welcome in their little garden house. They spoke German very well, having been refugees in Germany for awhile after having fled from the Russians in their homeland. Mrs. Meikup was the former secretary for the Estonian president. They made me feel so good in their little home, they couldn't do enough for me. They had no children and took me under their wings.

As it turned out, my husband was able to get all the papers for his immigration in New York without returning to Germany, because I was now in the USA as an official immigrant. It was a great help, thanks to my sponsor. My husband, Gerd, applied for his required internship at the Jersey City Regional Hospital and was accepted with open arms. We looked for an apartment nearby and found one on the Bay in Bayonne, waiting time three months. We had to rent an apartment in Hoboken. I was scared all the time in that neighborhood, but we couldn't afford anything better and I had to be close to NYC where I worked on 14th street. Many nights I couldn't sleep because of the bad neighborhood. My husband had to work many night shifts. In the meantime, I was introduced to the manager of Church World Service. He and his wife were from Germany and we became good friends. I was hired as a file clerk, but moved ahead fast as a translator, having had six years of English in a private school, thanks to my dear parents. The language came very handy. At this time, Church World Service took care of lots of Hungarian refugees, whose land was occupied by the Russians. They got out of their country with nothing but a suitcase and went to Germany for freedom. There they were in camps for a long time until we in Church World Service could find them sponsors. After that, they had to wait for their immigration papers, and then they would be stuffed into little ships like sardines.

My job was to be at the pier with many other workers to welcome these newly arrivals and greet them in the German language and bring them to assigned hotels for one day before getting them to their destinations. It was so sad to see them coming off the ship with their sparse belongings. They were so grateful being able to speak to me in German, a language they could manage. We had to put around their neck an identification -- their name, their sponsor's name and their destination. The next day, I had to pick up my group and put them into buses, trains or airplanes depending on the sponsor's address. They looked so scared to be left alone in a new country, not speaking the same language. Later on, I received some beautiful thank-you letters telling me how they got settled . Most letters were satisfying to read, but there were also some complaints that the sponsors were using them very badly. In such cases we had to check into the situation and find them different sponsors. All-in-all they were most grateful to have landed in a free world away from Communism.

Our apartment in Bayonne was small, two bedrooms, one bath, but we couldn't afford more with my husband's internship. Now we were able to think of our children's arrival and we started the applications for them to enter the USA. We were all so excited about it, getting the family together again. The waiting time for the entrance permit seemed endless , but finally we heard from my sister that everything came through in Berlin for Karin. Klaus in Vienna was still waiting. Mr. Hesse, the manager of Church World Service, offered to bring Karin over on the ship with his wife and children. That was a big relief for us. My brother-in-law took Karin to the ship and met Mrs. Hesse, who took over. My daughter was very, very close to my brother-in-law and the farewell was very hard. Here she was on a big ship with strangers, nine years old. She was so seasick; they got into bad weather, but finally we held her in our arms. It was so unforgettable to have her back with us in our new little home.

Taking her to school was scary. Since Karin couldn't speak English, she was put into a class with the little ones in first grade. Thank God, the children were nice to her. In the afternoons, she went outside with her roller skates and made friends in no time. After a few days, she told me not to pick her up from school; she wanted to take the bus with "all her friends."

They didn't have to keep Karin too long in first grade. They even jumped her up another grade; she was ahead of her same-age pupils. It surely didn't take her long to pick up English.

I was not able to stay home too long; my little income was the main thing we had with my husband going through two years of internships again. So here was my little sweet Karin, nine years old, with a key around her neck to come home to an empty nest. She didn't seem to mind it too much with all her new friends living close-by. Our Christmas with Karin was beautiful, but of course we did miss not having Klaus with us. However, his aunt in Vienna made his stay there also very pleasant for him. She was like a mother to him and had raised him in her home after her sister's death until my husband and I got married. Finally the visa came through and Klaus arrived a few months later and settled beautifully in school. He had a few lessons in English in Vienna to be prepared a little bit. Again, all the children were very kind to him.

All four of us took advantage of the freedom we had traveling as far as we felt like going without being stopped by the Russians. We went to the shore a lot on weekends, to "Avon by the Sea," or, on fall weekends, to the Catskill Mountains and on the first summer vacation to Maine. We are all nature lovers and had a great time hiking, swimming, and playing tennis.

Because the children had six to eight week long summer vacations, we sent them back to Berlin and Vienna, because we parents had to work. They had great times there seeing all the family together, and we could relax knowing they were in good hands.

It worked beautifully for several years until my sister in Berlin got in touch with us in 1961 and told us to get Karin out of Berlin as soon as possible: The Berlin Wall had begun to be built between West Berlin and its surrounding Soviet occupied territories. The family was afraid that they might get stuck behind the wall. We sent air mail tickets immediately and got her out of Berlin to return to us where she would be safe. The Berlin Wall was put up on August 13th, 1961.

Because of the irregular hours at work with lots of overtime our children were left alone quite often. My Karin got more and more sullen from day to day. Something was wrong. I talked to her alone. Although she was reluctant to talk at first for fear of further cruelty from Klaus, Karin did open up eventually. She shared that in the parents' absence Klaus, who was three years older than Karin, bossed her around and compelled her to do not only her own chores but his as well. He manipulated her physically and emotionally. She and I had noticed that the older Klaus got, the more he asked his father to do things for him and with him. He knew that he had his father under his control. It did hurt Karin and me a lot. Klaus would not listen to me any more. In my husband's mind was the promise to his dying wife to just live for his son. Klaus caught on to that and took advantage of it. After Karin confided with me how Klaus treated her, I waited for my husband to come home I confronted him with that situation. I asked him to move out with Klaus, to take everything he wanted to, no alimony or child support would be asked of him. I still don't know how I had the nerve to do that. With my salary alone I could not keep the apartment. At that time my husband had finished his internship and had a good income.

Well, he accepted my offer, moved out within a few days into an apartment across the courtyard from us, so we could see one another through the windows.

As much as I enjoyed working in Church World Service, the salary was not enough to support myself and Karin. So I took a day off from work and went from one company to another asking if they hired people. I was lucky: Air Reduction needed a file clerk and I was hired. At least I had my foot in the door and perhaps could work my way up eventually to the position of secretary.

One memory sticks with me of my time with Air Reduction. One manager showed me pictures of the Jewish people in the death camp at the time of their liberation by the Americans. He asked me how we could ever have let that happen. My answer was that we did not know anything about it. It seemed like a lie to him, but it was not. It was the best kept secret of the Nazi regime.

Even though I had meanwhile been promoted to secretary at Air Reductions, I tried to get as much overtime at work as possible to supplement our income. My daughter and I also babysat some nights. I began to sell copperware and jewelry on the side, Karin also took care of dogs. So we were able to make ends meet, and enjoy our peace at home.

On our first Christmas alone we could not afford a tree. When we looked across the courtyard we saw my husband's place beautifully decorated. My husband and I were on good speaking terms; he thought we might have a good life together after our children would have left for college. He had the nerve to ask me if he and Klaus could come over for Christmas dinner. My husband was lonely. He spoiled Klaus rotten, gave him a Mercedes when he was still in high school and plenty of money to spend. Neighbors told us that when Klaus had a date and picked up girls he had a bunch of roses to hand them. Everything first class! All my friends told me that I was stupid not to ask for alimony. I was too proud. I did ask him to move out and broke up our marriage for my daughter's sake. He had never adopted my Karin, so there was no responsibility for her on his part.

Karin and I did fine until she got into the wrong group in high school. The teacher called me: Karin skipped classes and forged my signature on reports. I was called to school and asked to go back to Germany with her. It hit me very badly.

I met through friends in Connecticut a German doctor who wanted to marry me and take Karin and me back to Germany. I was desperate and asked my husband for a divorce. He would not give it to me.

Karin eventually was doing fine. We did a lot of mother-daughter things together. In spite of just barely making ends meet, we enjoyed our life with friends. Eventually we could afford to take a few trips together.

I never will forget the time when I booked a cruise for Karin and myself to the Caribbean. Karin was in her last year in high school in Bayonne. I called the school and told them that Karin was sick and had to stay home for a week. They would never have let her go on vacation, and I could not get off from work any other time. Friends brought us to the ship in New York.

We were sitting on our suitcases at the pier waiting to go aboard when a photographer approached us and took a picture of us. He then asked for our address to send us the picture when we would return. What we did not know was that he put the picture into our local newspaper, - mother and daughter taking a trip to the Caribbean Islands. That did not go over too well at school.

My husband and I were separated for seven years, but we maintained good speaking terms most of the time. We even went on little trips together on weekends without the children. We still had feelings for each other, but for the children's sake the separation was necessary. Even on holidays, my husband and Klaus joined us; the kids got along fine in our presence. My husband was still hoping that we would have a life together once the children were on their own.

Dear neighbors of ours invited me one evening for dinner where I met John Faber who later was to become my husband. Our friends did try to match us up. We could not care less for each other, then. Their disappointment was great because they thought that we would make a great pair. John Faber had gone through a very painful divorce a half a year earlier, and apparently was not a person to stay by himself.

During the holidays, Karin and I always had big celebrations with friends. Easter came around and we invited some friends. Of course, I was asked to include John Faber, who was lonesome. He accepted. My husband also showed up and the two met. We all had a good time together.

A few weeks later I got a call from John Faber, asking me out for dinner. I accepted and we had a long talk about his life. I also opened up, talking about my situation not being able to get a divorce from my separated husband. It was a fascinating evening and John Faber was a very interesting man indeed. He was a photo journalist and worked for Eastman Kodak as a VIP-PR, representing the press. He had contact with all the well known people. He took me to one of the Press Parties, and I was amazed to notice how everybody came to us and told me how much John Faber was loved. Having been very reserved for all these years living by myself, I felt very comfortable being in his presence. His life had not been easy either. His parents had a bakery in Brooklyn where he grew up as an only child.

His parents were busy in the mornings in the store and he had to get his own breakfast which usually consisted of a cream pie. In spite of all the sweets he never had any problem with his teeth until the end of his fiftieth year, when he finally needed a filling.

It is sad that I never met his parents. It was a very loveable threesome, John and his parents, as I was told many times by John and surviving members of his family. His loving parents, besides working hard in their bakery, gave him all their love which he in turn gave to many, many others. As a teenager he had lost his beloved mother, and eventually his father married again, the stepmother being everything but nice. John went to college in Tuscaloosa, Alabama, and worked on the side as a photographer for the Birmingham News, where he eventually was hired. He had studied journalism and became the chief photographer for the newspaper. He met a lovely young lady from Birmingham. They got married and bought a nice home close to her parents to whom she was very attached. They had two lovely children, a son, John, and Marlene, their daughter.

One day he was approached by Eastman Kodak to start as a Press Representative in New York with a bigger salary and the possibility of climbing up the ladder in a big company like Kodak. A better future was ahead. He discussed it with his wife who agreed that he should accept this generous offer. John quit his news paper position in Tuscaloosa and went along to New York to look for a place to live in a pleasant area for his family to live when he would start his new job. He found a nice home in a lovely neighborhood in Denville, New Jersey, and settled there with his family.

John enjoyed his new job very much. Everything went well for a while.

One day, his wife told him that she didn't like living in the North. She wanted to go home to be near her parents. John was in shock. He tried everything to change her mind but was unsuccessful. Eventually his wife packed up her belongings and went home to her parent's house, taking the children with her. It broke John's heart to lose his family. Not long after that his wife divorced him.

John buried himself in his work. With the loss of his family still fresh, he was very vulnerable. At that time he met a woman who just had been divorced and was left with her little son. She was desperately looking for a husband who would support her and the little boy. She found just the right guy with a heart of gold, doing everything for everybody.

They got married and John adopted the little boy to build a family. Later on John and his wife had three more children on their own, two daughters and one son. Now his wife had all the security she had been looking for and began to show her real self. John had to travel a lot covering the press nationwide. When he used to come home, she would have her weekender packed to go and left John alone to fend for himself with the four children to take care of.

The marriage slowly fell apart. No matter how much John did, nothing was good enough. She pushed him around in every way. Eventually their marriage ended in divorce, but John stayed very close to his children in Alabama and New Jersey. He couldn't do enough for them. They did love their father very much.

When I met John he had been divorced for half a year. By that time he had moved into a condo on the Hudson river with a view of Manhattan, having left his house to his former family in order to stay close to his children. He.had just returned from a trip around the world with a friend of his. They had taken a lot of pictures and John wrote articles about his experiences in other countries illustrating them with his photos. These articles paid for the expenses of his travels. He also was a member of the Travel Writers' Assoc. so future trips did not cost him anything.

With all that background I opened my heart to him and we got together more often. John belonged to many different organizations and took me to some of the gatherings where I would meet interesting people all the time. Life for me became very fascinating; there was never a boring minute. John planned many a wonderful get-together.

John was still traveling a lot. He asked me to visit him in his condo one night, but I didn't want to be alone with him. Old fashioned German girl that I was, I played hard to get. So instead he gave me the key to his apartment and asked me to invite some other secretaries from my office at a time when he was traveling. He wanted me to see his place very badly. I was curious to find out why.

I went with my girlfriend, a coworker, after work to his apartment. The moment we stepped through the door we had a breathtaking view of Manhattan by night. It immediately drew us to the big picture window. It was indescribably beautiful. When we turned from the window we saw a note on the table to please order dinner on his account in one of the better restaurants

View from John's condo in New Jersey looking across the Hudson River at Manhattan

nearby. The table was set with candles and flowers, with another note that in the freezer were glasses for margaritas with salt around the rim, and in the fridge the drinks fully prepared. All we had to do is to enjoy them. My girlfriend and I were speechless. So much thoughtfulness!

My Karin, who lived with me in our apartment in Bayonne, was ready for high school graduation. John Faber joined us for the celebration. He shot nice pictures of the festivity.

Karin fell in love with a guy whom I could not stand. They planned the engagement. Thank God, I was able to talk to my future husband, who showed great interest in my daughter's and my relationship. He advised me to welcome this guy to our home and be kind to him. If I were to talk against him, Karin would turn around and marry him right away. I was fortunate to have had John as my advisor. I gave Karin and her guy a big engagement party in a nearby restaurant – a German tradition. I had to borrow money to do that, but it was worth it. All our friends joined us. We had a dinner dance party, and the pair got a lot of gifts. I was hoping that with this gesture they would not rush into marriage too fast. It worked!

Just one more of John's many, many thoughtful things that swept me off my feet: He was assigned to Atlantic City to be judge at the annual beauty pageant. He ordered tickets for his four children from his second marriage and for Karin and me, so that we could all meet one another. I insisted on paying my own way for Karin and myself. I had to be very firm because he wanted to treat us all the way, but I had learned meanwhile that most of his income went to support two wives and six children. We all went to a nice restaurant and Karin and I got to meet John's children. They were thrilled to meet my Karin, a teenager by this time, and we all had a good time together.

The next morning we rented bicycles, and on the bike John popped the question, "Will you marry me?" He knew that I was married. He had met my husband

and had learned from the Ellenbergers, who had brought us together, that my husband would never consent to a divorce. When I mentioned that to John, he said not to worry, when he wants something, he will make sure to work hard to get it. I told him, still riding our bikes, that I would only get married if I could have a child. He almost fell off his bike. There was no way for him to think of more children; six were quite enough. So we left that alone. He knew how important it was for me to have a family, to be able to raise a child with lots of love between husband and wife. I was thirty-eight years old; time was running out for me to have a baby.

John eventually gave in. But how were we to get married without a divorce from my husband? Our good friends, the Ellenbergers, who had brought us together and also, being neighbors of ours, knew my husband well suggested that they would help if needed. My husband thought a lot of the Ellenbergers.

One evening, John Faber called my husband to talk to him. My husband asked him to come to his office the next evening. John did. The doctor shone bright light into John's face. After the discussion had gone on for a while, the doctor put his hand under the desk and John thought for sure he was reaching for a pistol. (I had told John at an earlier time how my first husband almost came to a duel with my second over the issue of divorce). Instead there was a click from his tape recorder which was hidden under the desk; the doctor had taped the whole discussion. He adamantly refused to give in to a divorce, which I had known from the beginning. I was stuck. A few days later, the Ellenbergers had invited John and myself over for dinner. They had thought of a grand idea which was carried out a few days later. They invited my husband, Gerd, and Klaus for dinner . They told him that if he wouldn't sign the divorce papers, I would now insist on half of everything he owned plus alimony. Klaus did not like that idea at all. He wanted to inherit everything from his father. So he talked his father into signing the papers for the divorce – with nothing to give away. The Ellenbergers had obtained the papers from John's lawyer. The doctor signed them in front of Klaus without further consideration of the details. Anything Klaus wanted Klaus got! The Ellenbergers delivered the papers to John. He called his lawyer in Birmingham, Alabama, and the next morning John and I were on the plane to Birmingham. The lawyer, who was a member of the Ku Klux Klan and had a lot of power, met us at the airport, gave us the name of a hotel where we were to stay and wait for him to deliver the divorce papers to us. He had registered me to stay at the hotel for several weeks, to satisfy the legal requirement of minimum residency in a divorce case. He took the divorce papers to the courthouse and came back in the afternoon with my divorce all signed and sealed. When John was the chief photographer for the Birmingham News several years ago, he had a good working relationship with that lawyer. Since those days, the lawyer thought a lot of John and therefore was happy to be able to help him.

He congratulated us. John Faber insisted on getting married immediately, but there was a waiting period after a divorce. Instead the lawyer called one of his friends, a judge in Trenton, Georgia, and asked him to marry us the same day. We got his telephone number to call him and then rented a car and drove to Trenton. We arrived around 10 p. m. and phoned the judge who told us how to find the court house. When we got there, he was waiting for us with a witness to perform the marriage. We stood in front of him and he talked to us. I was overtired, did not understand one word he said (heavy Southern accent) and started to laugh. John, very embarrassed, looked at me, and I told him that I couldn't understand anything. He asked the judge to talk slowly and a few minutes later we were married. The judge handed us little bags with all kinds of things for newly-weds, and I laughed again.

We went to a hotel around 11 p.m. and asked to be awoken at 2 a.m. in order to catch the plane home to New Jersey. Around 6 a.m. we arrived at my apartment and woke up my Karin and told her that we got married. She was so happy for us. She said that shortly after we had left the morning before, the Doctor had come and wanted to talk about the papers he had signed. He had no idea what our plan had been when we left that morning and had tried to reach me in my office. I had taken the day off for the trip without telling anybody about our intention.

My new husband and I went each to our jobs the next day. We told everybody that we had got married. When the Doctor called me to request the return of the papers he had signed he was informed that I had gotten divorced and married, all in one day. All hell broke loose. My new husband had already bought a house for us in Mountain Lakes, N. J., a most beautiful area, some forty miles from New York City. That area was called the Oasis of New Jersey with its five lakes and pleasant woodland.

We planned to get married in our local church and have our children and close friends around us. My former husband, Dr. Klawitter, found out that we were planning a church wedding. He went from church to church in our new living area to find out where we might be registered. Finally he found the church and went to the pastor and told him that he could not marry us since I was not legally divorced. The pastor got in touch with us to check the story. After having seen the divorce papers and marriage certificate he was satisfied and we could go ahead with the plans for our church wedding.

Being legally married now, we went on our honeymoon to South America for four weeks. It was an unforgettable and beautiful experience. The trip was partly business and partly vacation. Otherwise, we could not have afforded it, since alimony for six children took a big chunk out of his salary. As a Kodak employee he could not take pictures in the U. S. A. and sell them to magazines; this would have been in conflict with his press customers. But as a travel writer, publishing stories about exotic places in other countries and illustrating them with his own photos for publications in travel magazines was no problem. But I was not worried about money. My marriage to John was pure, wonderful love.

A Final Note a Few Years Later

On my first husband's 90th birthday our daughter Karin and her 2 halfbrothers in Berlin planned a surprise party. Karin and the family asked me to join them in Germany. Being 85 years old and handicapped I had my doubts to fly overseas, but things worked out fine. I also invited my son and grandson to join us for a family reunion. It was wonderful. We stayed in Christel and Gerd's house and they spoiled us to no end.

Now we were ready for the surprise party. My ex-husband Ernst lives in a retirement home and the kids got a private dining room filled with flowers, table decorations and lots of great homemade cakes with plenty of champagne for toasting. And that we did ...a lot!

I came in late when everyone was seated already. I went right to Ernst and asked him if he remembered me. The answer was NO!

WHOOPS! I showed him our wedding picture and WHEW. He had a big smile and told all his family and friends, "Trudy was my first big LOVE". I was seated next to him with our Karin on his other side and we talked about good old times. Everybody was listening, interested to hear the part of our life together. All of a sudden he asked me why I left him. I did not want to answer that in front of all his friends and relatives, so I told him that I will answer the next day without anybody around. When it came to the end of the celebration he thanked us all for coming. He said he would never forget his 90th birthday. After saying good bye and hugging each other, he whispered in my ear, "I love you" and I did the same back. We hugged each other remembering some good times together with our sweet daughter.

Well, the next day he forgot his 90th birthday party. He has dementia and remembers the past very clear, but not the present. Thank God I didn't have to answer his question.

When it came to the final good bye, I told him that I would like to leave and let Karin stay alone with him for a while and I said, "Good bye, Gerd", instead of Ernst, not realizing it.

When Karin came out a few minutes later, she laughed so much and told me that after I left, he said, "Did you realize what your mother called me? Gerd!" That was my second husband's name who took me away from Ernst. I felt very bad but hope that the following day it was forgotten because of the dementia. I truly did not want to hurt him. I guess my age is showing too mixing up names.

Karin hands a shirt to her dad saying "SOMEONE IN VIRGINIA LOVES YOU"

When I visited Germany in 2011, Karin and I also went back to St. Nicholas Church where she and Christel were baptized after it had been rebuilt from the bombing. This is one of the oldest churches in Berlin-Spandau.

1945

Christel and Trudy in front of St. Nicholas Church

2011

In Gratitude

My profound gratitude to Karen Carter for being able to read my lousy handwriting in order to put it into the computer. My thanks for the patience doing it.

My big thank you also goes to Penny Finn having put all the pictures into the text. What another big job it was. The finished book was lying around for years by not knowing how to handle the pictures until dear Penny offered her help.

November 25, 2011

www.ingramcontent.com/pod-product-compliance
Ingram Content Group UK Ltd.
Pitfield, Milton Keynes, MK11 3LW, UK
UKHW041936190726
13854UKWH00004B/1613

9 781105 328466